THE BASILICA
OF THE
HOLY SEPULCHRE
OF
JESUS CHRIST
IN
JERUSALEM

G.S.P.Freeman-Grenville

CANA | CARTA
JERUSALEM

I know that my Redeemer lives,
  and that in the end he will stand upon the earth.
And after my skin has been destroyed,
  yet in my flesh I will see God;
I myself will see him
  with my own eyes — I, and not another.

Job 19.25–27

The angel said to the women, "Do not be afraid, for I know that you are looking for Jesus, who was crucified. He is not here; he has risen, just as he said. Come and see the place where he lay. ..."

Matt. 28.5–6

CONTENTS

FOREWORD

This short guide to the Basilica of the Holy Sepulchre of Jesus Christ in Jerusalem describes one of the most puzzling buildings in existence. Of all sacred buildings it has perhaps been worse treated by man than any other. Built by Constantine the Great as a 'house of prayer' to be 'an object of veneration to all' at 'the most blessed place of the Saviour's Resurrection,' it replaced a pagan temple erected on the site by the Emperor Hadrian. In the west it is generally spoken of as the Holy Sepulchre, but Greeks and Arabs still call it by its original name, the Church of the *Anastasis*, or Resurrection.

Constantine's edifice was badly pillaged by the Persians in 614. Respected by the Arabs when they evicted the Byzantines from Palestine in 638, it was razed to the ground by the insane Fatimid Caliph al-Hakim of Egypt in 1009. Restoration began in 1018, but by 1048 funds had only been found to rebuild a small part of what had once been a huge edifice, the part immediately surrounding the Edicule, or Tomb, of Christ. This the Crusaders extended by adding a typical twelfth century French church, and this combination is largely what is to be seen today.

It is shared by different rites, Armenians, Greeks and Latins (Franciscans), with lesser rights for Copts, Ethiopians and Syrian Jacobites. The story is long and complex, and raises many difficult questions. The restorations which began in 1967, and which are not yet wholly completed, have answered many of them. Most notable contributions have been made by the late Dame Kathleen Kenyon and by Fr Virgilio Corbo, OFM; on Calvary by Fr Florentino Díez Fernandez, OSA, whose work is only partly published, and by Professors G.Labbas and T.Metropoulos; and on the Edicule by Professor Dan Barag, of the Hebrew University, Jerusalem, and Professora Margherita Guarducci, of Rome. This work could not have been written without bringing their work under contribution.

It is divided into two parts, a historical introduction, and then a step by step description of the building as one goes round it. The writer knew it first more than forty years ago, when it was shored up and encumbered by supporting scaffolding. With memories of its awful disfigurement, it is with great joy that one sees that restoration has proceeded so far. Even so, much remains to be done: after thirteen more years since the completion of the rest, agreement has not yet been reached on the redecoration of the interior of the dome above the Rotunda, and—worse—the Edicule itself, held together by iron bands, is in fact disintegrating.

There are many to whom I owe a debt of gratitude, but most particularly to the late Very Revd Fr Dr José Montalverne de Lancastre, OFM, a former Superior of the Holy Sepulchre, Bro. Fabian Adkins, OFM, formerly Chief Latin Sacristan, the Rt Revd Bishop Guregh Kapikian, in charge of the Armenian excavations, Mr George Hintlian, Secretary to His Beatitude the Armenian Patriarch, the Revd Fr Florentino Díez Fernandez, OSA, and to Mr Shimon Gibson; and also to Mr Zev Radovan, who has been responsible for most of the photographs.

G.S.P.F.-G.

Sheriff Hutton,
York,
1 August 1993

The Basilica of the Holy Sepulchre

PART ONE: HISTORICAL

I. Calvary and the Resurrection

Carrying his Cross, Jesus went out to a 'place that is called Calvary, and in Hebrew Golgotha: there they crucified him.' In this all four evangelists agree, and St John adds that many Jews were able to read the title that had been set up on the Cross 'because it was near to the city.' This later St Paul confirms, that Jesus suffered outside the city gate 'that he might sanctify the people with his own blood.' In this place, St John says, 'there was a garden, and in this garden a new tomb in which no one had yet been buried.' There was a gardener, for when Christ had risen and appeared to Mary Magdalen, at first she thought he was the gardener. The tomb itself was closed by a revolving stone, an ordinary type of first century Jewish tomb. It was a very large stone, for when the women were on their way to the Tomb on the Resurrection morning, they said, 'Who will roll us back the stone? ...For it was very great.' It was the type of Jewish tomb known as an *arcosolium*, with an entrance vestibule leading to a chamber with a funerary couch within. The tomb itself was the property of a certain Joseph of Arimathaea, a wealthy member of the Sanhedrin, who had begged Pontius Pilate to let him bury Jesus' body.

Neither of these sites, that of Calvary or of the Tomb, were ever disputed until the second half of the nineteenth century. Since that time an immense amount of excavation has taken place, which has clarified the town plan of Jerusalem as it was in the first and second century AD. In 1967 excavations by Dame Kathleen Kenyon in the Muristan and by Dr Ute Lux at the Lutheran Church of the Redeemer beside the Holy Sepulchre showed that in the first century the site of the existing buildings lay outside the city, and was in fact a quarry. The present walls round the Old City were built in 1535–38 by the Ottoman Sulayman the Magnificent, and follow the line laid out for the Emperor Hadrian, when Jerusalem was refounded as Aelia Capitolina in AD 135. The quarry area showed no trace of occupation between the

Calvary, after D.Roberts, 1839

seventh century BC and AD 135, nor could Jewish tombs have been constructed there if it had been within the city walls, for this would have infringed Jewish law. The area, however, would seem to have been brought into the city between AD 40 and AD 44, when Herod Agrippa, grandson of Herod the Great, was allowed by Rome to rule much of his grandfather's kingdom. His short reign of four years was one of intense building activity. David's Jerusalem covered only 10.87 acres, Herod the Great's 140 acres; Herod Agrippa increased it to 310 acres. But not all of these were built over, as the excavations have shown. As even today on the north-east side of the Old City, and also in the part of the Armenian Quarter known as the Armenian Gardens, there was a certain proportion of cultivable land. Thus here, at the foot of Calvary, and in the garden where the Tomb was, vines, figs, carobs and olives may well have been grown.

The testimony of the Gospels and that of excavation agree with each other. No excavation could prove that the sites of Golgotha and of the Tomb are authentic. It shows, nevertheless, that they *can* be authentic. And this can be sustained from both pagan and from Christian sources.

II. The Temple of Jupiter

In AD 135 the Emperor Hadrian ordered the foundation of a new, pagan city on the site of Jerusalem. It was to be called Aelia Capitolina because his full name was Publius Aelius Hadrianus, and Capitolina because the city was to be dedicated to the three Roman deities worshipped in the Capitol in Rome, Jupiter, Juno and Minerva. As early as 132 he had wished to set up a statue of Jupiter in the Holy City, but his plan could not go ahead until Bar Kochba's revolt, which this had provoked, had been settled.

There was a standard Roman religious ceremony for the foundation of a city, known as the *pomerium*. It is certain that this ceremony was carried out in Jerusalem because it is attested by numerous commemorative coins that show the governor, Tinneius Rufus, ploughing the circuit of the city walls with an ox and a cow. More than 200 of these can be seen in the Flagellation Museum. Very detailed descriptions of similar ceremonies exist. They were carried out under the supervision of religious officials known as *augurs*. Their function was primarily to deduce the future from signs in the sky, and so to mark out, or *inaugurate*, the city in accordance with their observations. The centre of these cities was its temple, and its orientation was the special care of the *augurs*. Aelia Capitolina was no exception.

The site chosen for the Capitol temple in Jerusalem was where the Basilica of the Holy Sepulchre stands today. St Jerome tells us, c.385:

> From the time of Hadrian until the reign of Constantine for about 180 years there stood on the site of the Resurrection a statue of Jupiter; and on the rock of the Cross a marble statue of Venus was erected and worshipped by the heathen, the authors of the persecution believing that they might take our faith in

Coin of Aelia Capitolina

the Resurrection and the Cross away from us if they polluted the Holy Places with their idols.

Already more than fifty years before Eusebius of Caesarea had given an account of the site when Constantine's basilica was built. As Bishop of Caesarea, then the senior bishopric in Palestine, he was particularly well-placed to be accurately informed. It was he, with Bishop Makarios of Jerusalem, who had asked Constantine for the restoration of the Holy Places at the Council of Nicaea in 325. At their instance Constantine had ordered 'the most glorious site of the Resurrection' to be made 'manifest to all and venerable.' Above the 'cave of the Redemption' ... 'ungodly and impious persons' had 'determined to conceal the truth' by covering up the whole place. After raising it to a certain height, they paved it with stone, entirely concealing 'the Divine cave' under it. Then they built a shrine, in honour of Aphrodite, 'to offer their foul oblations on profane and accursed altars.' A contemporary of Jerome, and his friend, Paulinus of Nola, has a slightly different story, and places on Golgotha a statue of Jupiter.

Recent excavations as described by Fr Corbo show quite clearly that these descriptions are accurate in substance, even if there is some difference in particulars. The whole area of the quarry had been covered with earth, in such a way as to construct a gigantic terrace. Only the hillock of Golgotha was left uncovered, probably because it was not needed for the platform of Hadrian's temple. Fr Corbo has been able to make a hypothetical reconstruction of the entire building complex from Hadrianic fragments remaining on the site, most particularly in the Rotunda, in the Mary Magdalen

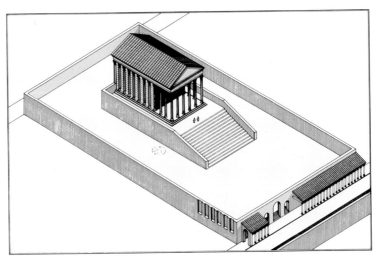

Reconstruction of the Capitol Temple

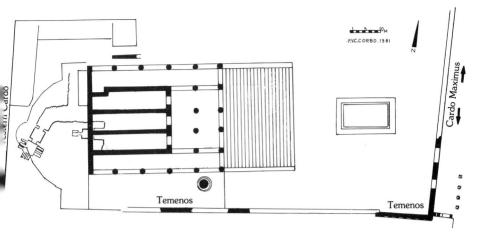

Hypothetical ground plan of the Capitol Temple, after Fr Corbo

chapel and between Calvary and the Choir. None of these are visible, but above ground there are very substantial remains to be seen in the Russian Alexander Hospice (see below, p.44), behind Zalatimo's sweetshop, where they can be seen through a hole in the wall, and in the Coptic Hospice, in the Khan ez-Zeit. All the remains are shown on page 45.

The street known as the Khan ez-Zeit was once the *Cardo Maximus*, the principal street of Hadrian's city. But it follows a line laid out by Herod Agrippa's builders, to whom this part of the city is due. Fr Corbo's plan, rather surprisingly, shows Hadrian's entrance not at right angles to it. It is not rectangular, as we would expect, but trapezoid in shape. There is no physical reason why this should be so, for the builders had an unencumbered space in which to lay out his temple. It follows, then, that the oblique lay-out in relation to the street is due to the *augurs*, whose decision it must assuredly have been.

The evidence for deliberate orientation does not end there. According to St Jerome Hadrian had two further statues erected, a statue of himself and also one of Jupiter on the site where the Jewish Temple had formerly stood. The *Chronicon Paschale* adds that Hadrian's own statue was placed where the Holy of Holies had formerly stood. The head of a statue generally believed to be that of Hadrian, now in the State Hermitage Museum, St Petersburg, found in Jerusalem in 1873, may well be from this statue. The Jewish rebellion that flared up in AD 132 was precisely because of the proposal to erect a statue of Jupiter in the Holy City. What more suitable site, then, after 135, when the rebellion had been crushed, for a statue of Hadrian than where the Jewish

Temple had stood, and, in particular, on the site of the Holy of Holies?

This has long been a subject of controversy. A conservative view places the former Temple in the *Haram al-Sharif*—the Noble Sanctuary—as the Arabs know it—that is, on Mount Moriah, or the Temple Mount, on or west of the site of the Dome of the Rock (commonly, but wrongly spoken of as the *Mosque of Omar*). More recently a number of scholars have sited it north of the Dome of the Rock, with the Holy of Holies on the site of the *Qubbat al-Arwa*, or *al-Alwa*, the Dome of the Spirits, or Tablets. The second name is suggestive of the Tablets of Stone of the Ten Commandments. The axis of a line drawn eastward from there passes through the southern half of the Golden Gate, the only gate of the *Haram* not reconstructed by Sulayman the Magnificent, and below which are remains possibly of the period of Solomon. The same line projected westward arrives precisely on Golgotha. Thus we may deduce that when the *augurs* performed the *pomerium*, they deliberately orientated the Capitol of Aelia Capitolina to agree with this axis, from Golgotha to the *Qubbat al-Arwa*, arguably the former Holy of Holies, whence to the Golden Gate. A further prolongation of this line would reach the traditional site on the Mount of Olives of the sacrifice of the Red Heifer, as described in the Book of Numbers and in the Midrash *Berakoth.*

Altar uncovered in the excavations on Golgotha

A bust of Hadrian (found near Beth Shean)

If these deductions from the actual site of Hadrian's temple are correct, the accusations made by Eusebius, Jerome and others that Hadrian was carrying out a deliberate policy of desecration of the sacred sites seems more than justified. But they need to be qualified. The policy of desecration was just as much directed against Jews as against Christians.

In the course of his excavations on Golgotha, Fr Florentino Díez Fernandez uncovered a small pagan altar of offering, with fragments of calcined bones and ash. Full publication is eagerly awaited, for much information can be recovered by analysis. Even so, his find firmly authenticates Eusebius and Jerome.

III. Constantine's Basilica

The earliest Christians can hardly have felt much interest in the Holy Places, for they lived in eager expectation of the Second Coming. When these hopes were not immediately realised, and when, at the same time, Christian tradition and the books of the New Testament gradually crystallized, so the Scriptures became more deeply searched. The first of whom we have record, Melito of Sardis, distinguished as a Bishop and as a theologian, went to Palestine to inquire about the canon of the Old Testament so as 'to provide extracts from the Law and the Prophets in so far as these apply to our Redeemer and to our faith as a whole.' This was c.170. In 212 another bishop, Bishop Alexander, came to Jerusalem 'to pray and visit the Holy Places.' He founded a library, that is, a house of study, in Jerusalem, of which later he was elected Bishop. Shortly after there came Origen, the greatest theologian of the early Church (185–254). It was not until the reign of Constantine that pilgrimage became common. Even then, at the end of the fourth century, St Gregory of Nyssa remarked tartly: 'There is no need to make a pilgrimage, for "the Kingdom of God is within you".' St Jerome was of a similar mind: 'It is not praiseworthy to have been in Jerusalem, but rather to have lived virtuously in Jerusalem.'

Eusebius' *Life of Constantine* gives a detailed account of the recovery of the sacred sites of the Resurrection and of Golgotha, and of the building of the basilica. It is written with all the high-flown rhetorical style that was customary among the pagan orators and Christian preachers of the day. The discovery of the 'venerable and hallowed monument of our Saviour's resurrection' was 'contrary to all expectation': quite possibly it was thought that Hadrian's workmen had demolished the tomb rather than having simply covered it up. No doubt the site was well-known enough in local Christian tradition. Constantine's edict ordered 'that a house of prayer worthy of God should be erected ... on a scale of rich and imperial costliness.' Provincial governors throughout the east were ordered to make 'liberal and abundant grants.' In Jerusalem Bishop Makarios was sent an Imperial Letter. The building was to 'surpass all the churches in the world in the beauty of its walls, columns and marbles.' The bishop was given *carte blanche* to procure them from anywhere he chose. He was to use his own judgement in the design, and especially whether there should be a coffered ceiling. He

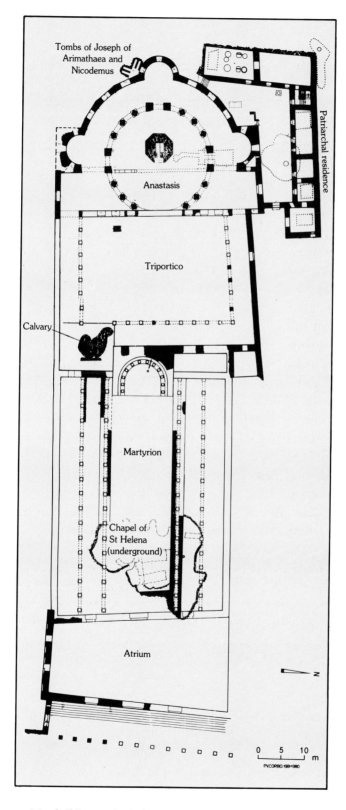

Constantinian buildings at the Holy Sepulchre, after Fr Corbo; remains shown in black

Aerial view of the Holy Sepulchre compound; (centre) *the basilica and* (left) *the Deir al-Sultan*

was to inform the local authorities of his needs in workmen and specialist tradesmen, and to report to the Emperor, not forgetting his needs in marbles and columns, and his views on the coffered ceiling. If this was his choice, then it was to be ornamented with gold. As to the Tomb itself, it was to be beautified with much ornament, and decorated with all kinds of adornments. Doubtless, Constantine would have had in mind an Imperial tomb, decorated with marble and mosaic.

Although Eusebius says that all traces of Hadrian's temple were removed, it is clear that there was considerable re-use of materials. The Tomb itself was freed completely from the rubble on which Hadrian's temple had been built, and from its surrounding rock, so that it stood clear. On the rest of Hadrian's platform walls were now sunk to take the weight of a much heavier building. There was an entrance *atrium*, or courtyard, abutting on the *Cardo Maximus*, open to the sky. Then came a basilica with a nave and two aisles on each side. Roofed in lead, inside it had carved panel work, overlaid throughout with gold, which made the whole building glitter with rays of light. This church, with an altar set in the chord of the apse, with seating for the officiating clergy, was known as the *Martyrion*. Beyond it lay a second *atrium*, with colonnades on three sides, that is, a *Triportico*. Open on the western side the Edicule of the Tomb of Christ was now visible. It was surrounded by a domed Rotunda, supported by six piers and twelve columns. Outside the piers and columns was an unencumbered ring, with three apses, that could form a processional way (see plan, p.15).

Unfortunately Eusebius stops short and fails to describe the Edicule itself. There are no early literary descriptions of it. But its shape is known in a general way from numerous glass pilgrim flasks that have survived in different places, and in which pilgrims carried home holy oil in memory of their pilgrimage. These are of the sixth century. There is a single earlier representation in the form of an ivory reliquary, which for long was preserved at Samagher, near Pola, in Istria. The various scenes carved on its sides, back and cover enable its representation of the Edicule to be dated with precision at AD 439. It had been cut free from virgin rock, and was octagonal, with an octagonal dome surmounted by a Cross.

Outside the basilica proper were two further groups of buildings. On the north side, where the Franciscans now have their quarters, was the Patriarchate, with residences for the Patriarch and his clergy. On the south side of the church, where the present entrance courtyard is, are three chapels, one with the remains of the Crusader tower behind. They replace what was originally a baptistery. We can only

Ivory reliquary from Samagher showing the Edicule

Latin Easter ceremonies

surmise what the original plan was, for they have never been
examined archaeologically.

They may provide one interesting clue. We have very few
details of the Jerusalem liturgy in early times. It was greatly
admired by a pilgrim nun, Egeria, who visited Palestine,
Egypt and much of the Middle East, c.384. She tells us far
too little. For the baptismal ceremonies at Easter, however,
the *Catachetical Lectures* of St Cyril, Bishop of Jerusalem,
composed c.347, seem to preserve something of the liturgical
context. These lectures were delivered in Lent to catechumens,
new believers seeking Baptism, three lectures in each of six

weeks. They were delivered in the Baptistery, where, during the Easter Vigil, the rite of Baptism was administered. Egeria tells how, after the ceremony of Baptism, the bishop and the newly baptized proceeded straight to the Edicule. Only after Baptism were the newly baptized admitted to the 'mysteries', the supreme mystery of the Eucharist. It is this with which the twenty-third lecture is concerned. It culminates in an oratorical climax with the great scene from the Apocalypse (4.2–11), with Christ in Glory, *Christos Pantocrator*, Christ the Sovereign of All, with the Four Living Creatures and the Twenty-Four Elders, as they cast down their golden crowns and cry: 'Holy, holy, holy is the Lord God Almighty, who was, and is, and is to come.'

In 1882, when the baroque decorations were stripped from inside the dome of the Imperial Chapel at Aachen (Aix-la-Chapelle), which Charlemagne had modelled on the Rotunda of the Holy Sepulchre in 796, it was precisely this scene that was disclosed. Was it, in fact, that Charlemagne knew that this was the scene depicted in the dome above the Edicule? It might seem a very plausible explanation of his choice. For we do not know what decoration was destroyed when the dome was severely damaged by the earthquake of 810.

Underground

Under Constantine's basilica are a number of cisterns and, not far from the Edicule, an underground chamber that may have been the *favilla*, the depository for the remains of offerings, of Hadrian's temple. Under the *Martyrion* was a crypt, known by the Crusaders as the Chapel of St Helena, and, now in Armenian possession, as the Chapel of St Gregory the Illuminator. From this a staircase leads down to the Chapel of the Finding (Latin, *Inventio*, and so Invention) of the Cross. These stairs are partly eleventh century, partly of Crusader times. Here, according to tradition, St Helena, the mother of Constantine the Great, found the Cross of Jesus and those of the two thieves. When it was excavated, what was evidently a disused cistern was disclosed within the earlier quarry; it contained debris of masonry of Roman, Byzantine and Crusader times. This is open to visitors, and where Mass is celebrated on the Feast of the Invention, or Finding, of the Cross (below, p.69).

Concealed behind the left hand altar in the Armenian chapel is a door, always kept locked, which leads to another part of the same cistern, but separated from it by a wall.

Here there are visible the foundation wall of the north arcade of Constantine's church, with a water drain intact, and the naked walls of part of the quarry. In this area pottery has been found of date between 63 BC and AD 350, but for certain it was covered up after Hadrian's temple platform had been built in 135. It is here that a famous *graffito*, known as the Jerusalem ship, has been found, with the inscription *DOMINE IVIMUS*. The script is of the third to fourth centuries, and the type of ship of the same period. The stratigraphy of the pottery, however, is of the first half of the fourth century, when Constantine's basilica was being built. This would have covered it once again. The inscription seems to be an allusion to the Pilgrim Psalm 121 (122), and so it may be ascribed to a pilgrim of the time when the church was being built. *Permission to visit this area may be sought from the Armenian divan* (below, p.55) *and is not always available. The space is so confined that it cannot be visited by large parties.* Recently an altar has been erected in it, dedicated to St Vartan, the first Christian King of Armenia.

Drawing of ship and the inscription DOMINUS IVIMUS

Calvary

The little hillock of Calvary, or Golgotha, was covered by a shrine wholly separate from Constantine's basilica. All the western half of the platform is an extension built in Crusader times, no doubt to accommodate a greater number of pilgrims. Here, as we have seen, under Hadrian there was a shrine in honour of Aphrodite, with an altar of

Greek altar at the 12th Station—the place of Crucifixion

offering. In 1990 Professor George Labbas, of the University of Thessalonica, excavated the area of the Greek altar of Calvary, exposing the virgin rock on which the Crucifixion took place, and displaying it beneath plate glass. It is in restrained good taste. Behind it an arch was disclosed, which has now been covered up again, which may be a relic of the Constantinian shrine on Calvary. Excavation has also taken place in the Chapel of Adam below Calvary, disclosing an apse which presumably belonged to the Constantinian building. It is thus difficult to conjecture what its appearance

Latin Good Friday procession

may have been, but a long description of the Good Friday
ceremonies is given by Egeria in her *Pilgrimage*. Golgotha
was surmounted by a Cross, and here the Bishop sat behind
a table, holding the Wood of the Cross and the Title. The
faithful came one by one, to kiss and venerate it. Between
mid-day and 3 p.m., she says,

> readings took place in the very spacious and beautiful
> courtyard between the Cross and the Anastasis (i.e. the
> Edicule). The readings are all about what Jesus suffered,
> from the Psalms, the Apostles (the Epistles or Acts) and
> from the Gospels. At 3 p.m. they have the reading from
> St John's Gospel about Jesus giving up his Spirit. Then
> a prayer is said, and the people are dismissed.

IV. Byzantines, Persians, Arabs, and Charlemagne

Constantine's Basilica was dedicated with great solemnity on 14 September 335 in the presence of the Emperor, although he was still unbaptized. Ever since this has been kept as a feast day, the Feast of the Exaltation of the Holy Cross. At the same time it represented an adaptation of the ancient Jewish Feast of the Tabernacles, which, like this solemnity, lasted for eight days. When Egeria was in Jerusalem c.384 this festival, known as the *Encaenia*, or Commemoration, was kept with especial magnificence, as 'the very date when the Cross of the Lord was discovered.' For it monks and others gathered from Mesopotamia, Syria, Egypt and the Thebaid as well as from other provinces. 'Although bishops,' she says, 'are few and far between, they never have less than forty or fifty in Jerusalem at the same time, accompanied by many of their clergy.' The liturgy was celebrated by the Bishop of Jerusalem in Greek, never in Syriac, 'so that everyone can understand what he means.' For those who only knew Latin, there were always some brothers or sisters who speak Latin as well as Greek to 'explain things to them.' Later pilgrims in the fifth century tell us little beyond that it was a scene of tranquil piety.

On 20 May 614 the Persian army sent by Khusrau (Chosroes) II invaded Palestine and sacked and pillaged the cities. They sacked Jerusalem with especial ferocity, and churches and religious buildings were pillaged and burnt. They seized the Wood of the Holy Cross, and carried it back to their capital at Ctesiphon, not far from the present Baghdad. Here, according to one tradition, Chosroes seated himself upon a golden throne, with a dove to represent the Holy Spirit, and, with the Cross on one side, and had prayers addressed to him blasphemously as God the Father.

By 628 the Emperor Heraclius had reconquered the lost eastern provinces from the Persians, and Modestus, Abbot of the Monastery of St Theodosius, was able to restore the basilica. It is not clear how much damage had been done, but possibly little harm had been done to the structure. For all was ready when Heraclius entered Jerusalem in the following March, and carried the Wood of the Cross back through the Golden Gate. But peace was not to be for long. The Prophet Muhammad died in 632. By 634 the Arabs, united now by Islam, burst out of the desert, and took all Palestine, and parts of Mesopotamia. By 636 they had all Syria and Iraq. In 638 they took Jerusalem. The Caliph 'Umar shortly visited it, and was conducted round the Holy Sepulchre. He refrained from praying in it deliberately, lest it be turned into a mosque, praying outside where now there is a mosque on the south side of the church. Christians were required to pay a poll tax like other non-Muslims, Jews and Zoroastrians. Since the tax was lower than that payable under the Byzantines, there was some advantage in the change of government. It was not Muslim policy to molest those of other faiths, and life proceeded tranquilly much as before. Arculf, a Bishop from Gaul, visited Palestine later in the century, and gave an account of his pilgrimage to Adomnan, Abbot of Iona. He makes no mention of the Arab presence at all. The same is the case with a number of other writers in the seventh and eighth centuries. It was in accordance with a decree allegedly promulgated by the Caliph 'Umar, which, even if spurious, makes the position clear:

> In the name of God, the Merciful, the Compassionate: This is the writing of 'Umar son of Khattab to the inhabitants of Jerusalem. I affirm that you [Christians] will have absolute security for your lives, your property

Reconstruction of the Edicule, after an ampulla, *c.500*

Gold ring decorated with a model of the Edicule, found in a 6th century building S of the Temple Mount

and your churches; and that they will not be inhabited by the Muslims, nor destroyed, unless you should rebel against us.

No other document exists concerning the Holy Sepulchre or any other Holy Place.

In 746 there was a disastrous earthquake, and again in 810. The last so damaged the dome of the Rotunda that wood had to be brought from Cyprus to restore it. Somewhat earlier diplomatic exchanges took place between the Caliph Harun al-Rashid and the Emperor Charlemagne. In Baghdad Charlemagne's ambassadors received for him a reliquary of the Holy Cross, a banner and the keys of the Holy Sepulchre, which might appear to be recognition of his protection of Christian pilgrims. What these exchanges meant in reality is debatable. Certainly in 935 Muslims—for the first time—occupied part of the *atrium* of the Holy Sepulchre for use as a mosque. There was further trouble in 966, when the victorious Byzantine Emperor Nicephorus Phocas retook Cilicia and part of Syria, and expelled the Arabs. They retaliated in Jerusalem by setting on fire the roof of the basilica, the Triportico and the Rotunda.

In 969 the Fatimids, in origin a Berber dynasty from faraway Morocco, but claiming descent from the Prophet's daughter Fatima and her husband Ali, seized Cairo and then Syria and Palestine. The earlier Fatimids were tolerant, if not

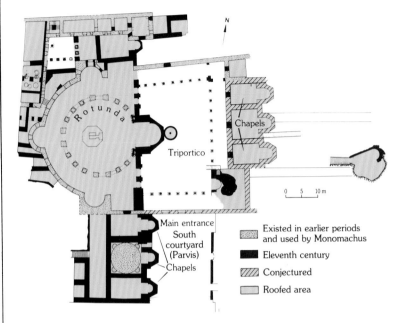

Plan of the 11th century basilica

indifferentist, in religion, but in 996 there succeeded as Caliph al-Hakim bi-Amr-Illah, a fanatic who persecuted women, Christians, Jews, and even his fellow-Muslims, with impartial venom and ferocity. In 1008, having laid heavy taxes upon pilgrims, he forebade the Palm Sunday Procession from the Mount of Olives. In 1009 he ordered the total destruction of the Holy Sepulchre, and this began on 25 August. Even the Edicule was destroyed and the funeral couch damaged. In 1012 the devastation was halted, it is said through the intercession of his mother, who was a Christian. By then even the pillars of the Rotunda had been reduced to mere stumps.

His successor gave permission for restoration in 1018, but funds were hard to find, and real work was begun only with the accession of Constantine IX Monomachus (1042–55). It took six years. The Edicule was rebuilt, and the Rotunda and its dome reconstructed. On its eastern side an arch was built and an apse, in which the altar was placed. The Triportico and the *Martyrion* remained in ruins. Funds were short, and the local clergy would doubtless have liked to do more. But they had done their best.

In the years that followed immediately the incursions of the Seljuq Turks rendered all Palestine unstable, and made regular pilgrimages all but impossible. It was this situation that led to the Crusades.

V. *The Crusader Basilica*

The Crusaders entered Jerusalem under Godfrey de Bouillon on 15 July 1099. They had massacred the Muslim inhabitants, and others had fled. So had the clergy. In this context it was intelligible that Latin clergy should replace the Greeks, and the Latin *praedominium*—overlordship—was to outlast the departure of the Crusaders after Saladin had defeated them at the Battle of the Horns of Hattin in 1187.

Immediately in 1099 Godfrey de Bouillon appointed Canons, who in 1114 became officially 'Canons of the Holy Sepulchre of our Lord Jesus Christ in Jerusalem,' to recite the daily Office in the Latin rite. A separate rule was drawn up for them in 1114, and the institution recognized by Pope Callistus II in 1122. Their constitution defined the object of the order as the praise of God for the gift of the Redemption and to sing the glory of the Resurrection of the Saviour. They wore black habits with a leather belt, and a white rochet and a black mantle with a patriarchal cross on the left shoulder in choir.

The small church of Constantine IX Monomachus was insufficient for their needs, both for the Office and for accommodation. An extensive building programme took until 1149, when the new church was consecrated. The eastern apse of the Rotunda was demolished, although its foundations, uncovered during recent excavations, still remain. The area

Royal Crusader seal of Jerusalem showing the city's three major landmarks: (left to right) *the Holy Sepulchre, the Citadel and the Dome of the Rock*

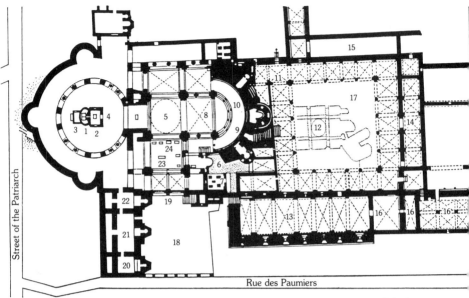

1. The Holy Sepulchre; 2. Chapel of the Angel; 3. Altar; 4. Rotunda; 5. Dome; 6. Golgotha; 7. Chapel of the Raising of the Cross; 8. Choir of the Augustinian Canons; 9. Stairs to the Crypt of St Helena; 10. Stairs to the Augustinian cloister; 11. Entrance to the cloisters; 12. Dome of the Crypt of St Helena; 13. Refectory; 14. Chapter Room; 15. Dormitory; 16. Kitchen, office, stores; 17. Cloister quadrangle; 18. Southern atrium; 19. Main entrance to the Basilica; 20. Chapel of St James; 21. Chapel of St John, former Baptistery; 22. Chapel of the Forty Martyrs; 23. Stone of Unction; 24. Royal tombs

Plan of the Basilica of the Holy Sepulchre and Priory of the Canons Regular of the Holy Sepulchre, after Frs Vincent and Abel

of the Triportico was re-used to build a conventional twelfth century French choir with an ambulatory containing three chapels. Calvary had its platform doubled in size and was incorporated into the main building.

Behind the ambulatory was a large chapel dedicated to St Helena. Originally it was the crypt of Constantine's church; it was now reached by stairs from the ambulatory. It had been reconstructed with older materials of different dates. Substantially it is what one sees now. Further stairs, in St Helena's Chapel, led down to the quarry and the cistern in which the crosses had been found.

The roof of the chapel was almost on a level with the floor of the *Martyrion*, which now became a four-sided cloister. In its centre the dome of the Chapel of St Helena projected, just as we can see it now. On the south side of the cloister there was a refectory with six windows and seven bays. At its eastern end were the kitchen and storerooms. On the east side of the cloister was a rather narrow chapter room, with small rooms at either end. The dormitory was at the same level on the north side; apparently all these buildings were single-storied only. The ruins of much of them can still be seen, but not very clearly, because the space is largely occupied by the dwellings of the Ethiopian monks, which have been built among them like an Ethiopian village.

A new entrance to the basilica was now constructed on its south side, with a bell tower in its north-west corner. This tower still stands, but with its two top storeys missing, giving it a squat, disproportionate appearance. The entrance had two doors, one of which was later walled up by Saladin. Above them was an elaborately carved tympanum with scenes from the Gospels. The best preserved is of the Raising of Lazarus. In 1927 it was decided to remove the whole tympanum to the Rockefeller Museum because it was so damaged by the weather.

Although the Latins now had the *praedominium*, the

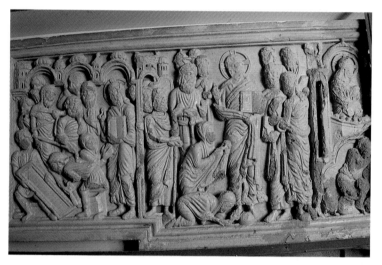

Carved tympanum of S doorway with scenes from the Gospels: (top) *the Raising of Lazarus and* (below) *the Last Supper (Rockefeller Museum)*

Crusader capitals at the entrance to the basilica

maximum liberty was allowed to other rites, including all the orientals, whether in communion with Rome or not. At great festivals the oriental clergy celebrated along with the Latins, and this practice can only have come to an end after 1582. In that year the Gregorian Calendar was promulgated in the west, so that Easter and other festivals came to be celebrated on different dates from the orientals, who continued to adhere to the Julian Calendar—as they still do.

On 5 July 1187 this state of affairs was ended by Saladin's victory at the Horns of Hattin. He arrived in Jerusalem on 2 October, and on the following day his army occupied all the Holy Places. He ordered the doors of the Holy Sepulchre to be closed for three days. All men, whether Christian or Muslim, were forbidden to approach it. The bells were removed from the tower: the Prophet Muhammad had hated bells. One of the two doors was walled up. Shortly, a Muslim doorkeeper was installed. Saladin, it is recorded, ordered that no Christian community should have the *praedominium*. That he now reserved for himself.

VI. Under the Ayyubids and Mamluks

The victor over the Crusaders, Saladin, was a Kurd by origin, and his correct name Salah bin Ayyub. It is from his father's name that the dynasty he founded is called Ayyubid. While owing a nominal allegiance to the Caliph in Baghdad, and with Saladin himself enjoying a certain hegemony, the Caliphate was divided among different members of the Ayyubid family, brothers, sons, cousins, ruling contemporaneously at the capitals of different provinces, with the title *Sultan*. Amongst these Egypt was the most important, and here, as elsewhere, the Ayyubids had as their principal military force *Mamluks*, chiefly Kipchaq Turks recruited from Central Asia as slaves, converted to Islam, and educated in all the military arts. Without family ties, their only focus of loyalty was to their masters. As they rose in the service, so generally they were manumitted, but the ties of loyalty remained. In Cairo they were quartered on an island in the Nile (Arabic: *Bahr al-Nil*), and thus their regiment was known as Bahri. After the decline of the Ayyubids in the mid-thirteenth century, the sultanate became elective among the Bahri Mamluks. Their dynasty was supplanted in the late fourteenth century by the Mamluks quartered in the Cairo citadel (Arabic: *Burj*), whence they were known as the Burji Mamluks. Most of these were of Circassian origin, and often cradle Christians, from what today is the mountainous region between modern Turkey and the former U.S.S.R. This second Mamluk dynasty was to last until the Ottoman conquest in 1516–1517. Thus from the twelfth century to the sixteenth the Holy Places were in the hands of rootless military rulers and converts to Islam.

Shortly after Hattin the Emperor Isaac Angelus obtained from Saladin permission for Greek clergy to return to the Holy Sepulchre. In 1192 Richard I Coeur de Lion of England secured a treaty with him for the free passage of pilgrims from the west with permission for two priests and two deacons of the Latin rite to reside in the Holy Sepulchre. The monastic buildings of the Augustinians had been handed over to the Copts, who still reside in what now is called *Deir al-Sultan*, the Sultan's Monastery, in some parts that still remain. Pilgrims, nevertheless, were heavily taxed, and the offerings on which the Holy Places depended were thus diminished. By 1217 the Church of the Lord's Sepulchre and the place

Priest in the Coptic monastery

of his Passion was without lamps, without honour, without respect, and always shut; it was opened only occasionally after offerings by pilgrims. A report of 1226 states that two Muslim custodians divided the proceeds between them. In 1229 the Holy Roman Emperor, Frederick II (1218–38), succeeded in obtaining a treaty from Sultan al-Malik al-Kamil that recognized him as King of Jerusalem, with Bethlehem and Nazareth, and in 1230 Alberto de Robertis celebrated Mass in the Holy Sepulchre as Papal Legate. The Augustinians now returned, only to be expelled again in 1239. A further treaty enabled their return in 1241, only to die in 1244, when all the Christians, Greek as well as Latin, were massacred by the Khwarismian Turks. It was in a fruitless endeavour to recover the Holy Places that Louis IX attacked Egypt in 1249, only to lose his life and have his army dispersed the following year. Shortly the Mongols invaded the Near East, further confusing the situation. Only by 1266 was some sort of order restored, and oriental and western pilgrims allowed to revisit the Holy Places. This was allowed only on payment to the Muslim custodians.

In 1346 the Franciscan Order had replaced the Augustinian Canons. Now for several centuries they lived on peaceful terms with the clergy of other rites: Armenians, Copts, Ethiopians, Georgians, Greeks and Syrian Jacobites. By the fifteenth century numerous writers witness that a pilgrim tourist trade was well established. Conventions of relations between Christians and Muslims had developed, and the latter were content enough so long as they could extort dues. For the pilgrims it was nevertheless a journey full of uncertainty and discomfort, with the Mamluks extracting the most in gratuities from their luckless victims. In 1480 and again in 1483 Fr Felix Faber, OP, made two pilgrimages. In the basilica the pilgrims were received by the Franciscans in procession, and mounted to Calvary singing the hymn *Vexilla Regis* as they still do now. They spent three nights of vigil in the church, much plagued with fleas 'jumping all about the pavement.' Not less were they plagued by merchants, selling cloth as well as objects of piety. Felix was distracted by the Jacobite priests beating on pieces of thin, polished iron (the *synambres* that had taken the place of bells) and by the shouts and strange cries of the Eastern Christians. But some pilgrims were no better. They spent the nights swilling wine and talking of worldly things, princes, quarrels, campaigns and warriors.

VII. From the Ottoman Turkish Conquest to Modern Times

If the conditions of all the communities in the Holy Sepulchre had been only just tolerable under the Mamluks, the Ottoman Turkish conquest, of Syria and Palestine in 1516, and of Egypt in 1517, spelt the beginning of a new era. The Ottomans were prepared to treat their subject peoples with tolerance, so long as they accepted clear and unarguable conditions. These later came to be known as the *Status Quo*, an abbreviation of a conventional diplomatic phrase, *status quo ante bellum*, the state of things before the war. In this case the reference was to the Crimean War, although the phrase is often used for conditions that obtained before that.

By conquering Constantinople in 1453 the Ottoman Turks had brought the Greek Byzantine Empire to an end. Greeks, Greek Orthodox by religion, formed however a high proportion of the population within the Ottoman Empire, and to a great extent dominated the Ottoman civil service. The fundamental strength of the Ottomans came to rest upon the corps of Janissaries, recruited exclusively from Christian villages, enslaved and converted to Islam. In such circumstances it was natural that the Greeks and other oriental churches, whose members were all Ottoman subjects, should now find themselves in a more favourable position than they had enjoyed under the Mamluks; on the contrary, the Latins, from the nations of western Europe with which the Ottomans were frequently at war, and in particular Venice, saw their influence decline. It was thus that there came into

Greek Orthodox Patriarch entering the church for Easter ceremonies

Chapel of St Abraham in the Greek Orthodox monastery

being what came to be known as 'the Eastern Question', which kept the question of the Holy Places in the forefront of world politics until well into the twentieth century. The first occasion on which the Ottomans used their power was the ejection of the Franciscans from the *Coenaculum*, the place in which the Last Supper traditionally had taken place, and giving it into Muslim hands, on the grounds that the tombs of David and Solomon, revered alike by them and the Jews, were there.

Further strength accrued to the Greeks in 1662, when the

Ethiopian courtyard

Patriarch Dositheos re-organized Orthodox institutions in the Holy Land, and founded the Confraternity of the Holy Sepulchre. Henceforward this operated as a governing body for the Greeks, with every facility that Ottoman subjects could enjoy. As to the Latins, as the seventeenth century wore on, so the influence of Venice, long the predominant European power in the region, steadily waned as a result of its wars with Turkey. France attempted to redress the balance through its ambassador at the Sublime Porte, where the Ecumenical Patriarch of Constantinople lived as the head of the largest of the Christian communities. In 1604, 1673 and again in 1740 Capitulations (so called because the agreement was drawn up in *capitula*, chapters) confirmed the rights of the Franciscans in the possession of Calvary and of the Holy Sepulchre, the Basilica at Bethlehem, and the Church of the Assumption of the Blessed Virgin in Gethsemane. On the other side, the Greek Orthodox Patriarch of Jerusalem had obtained a *firman* (decree) in his favour in 1637, and finally in 1757. His position was enhanced by the Treaty of Küchük Kainarji in 1774, in which Russia assumed protection of all the Ottoman Sultan's Orthodox subjects. All these changes were procured not on their merits but at considerable profit to the Sultan's treasury. It was not the Latins alone that suffered. Whereas in earlier times the seven communities (see above, p.33) arranged the cycle of sharing the Holy Sepulchre and other rights with one another, the poorer communities now dropped out or lost ground. The Georgians disappeared from Jerusalem altogether. The Ethiopians were excluded

Syrian Orthodox chapel

from the interior of the Holy Sepulchre, and banished to the roof above the Chapel of St Helena, for failure to provide the bribes that were openly canvassed. The Copts remained in possession of a lean-to chapel behind the Edicule, and the Syrian Jacobites retained only the use of an apse behind the Rotunda on Sundays and certain festivals. The Armenians, who had charitably sheltered the Latins when they were excluded from the Coenaculum, possessed only the Chapel of St Helena (now of their national saint, Gregory the Illuminator) and a chapel in the Rotunda gallery. The Crusader choir became an exclusive possession of the Greeks, while the Latins retained possession of the Chapel of St Mary Magdalen, of the Appearance of Jesus to his Mother, and the so-called Arches of the Virgin, together with the cistern Chapel of the Finding of the Cross. The Edicule of the Tomb of Christ remained in common, but with defined rights in it of the Armenians, Greeks and Latins as the three major communities.

Thus, at the end of the eighteenth century, Greek influence was paramount. This was facilitated by events in Europe, where the French Revolution had proscribed the Church and all religion, and put all Europe in a turmoil of war. In 1808 a disastrous fire burnt down the dome of the Rotunda and the dome and roofs of the Greek choir. The Edicule was unharmed, and this some regarded as miraculous. The Russian government found $2^1/_2$ million roubles to obtain permission to repair the building, and $1^1/_2$ million roubles for the actual repairs, huge sums for those days. It was in

Armenian Lent ceremonies in the Rotunda

this way that a partly rebuilt Edicule in a nineteenth century style replaced that of the eleventh century reconstruction of Constantine IX Monomachus, with a new dome which had to be reconstructed twice in the nineteenth century. At the same time high walls were built round the hitherto open Crusader choir, to support the dome above it. The Greeks also removed all trace of the tombs of Godfrey de Bouillon and of the Latin Kings. The only tomb that remained was that of an English Crusader, Philippe d'Aubigny, and that fortuitously, because the bench on which the Muslim doorkeepers habitually sat outside the entrance was on top of it. It was just before this event that Chateaubriand visited the Holy Places. He copied two of the inscriptions:

> *HIC JACET INCLYTUS DUX GODEFRIDUS DE*
> *BULION, QUI TOTAM ISTAM TERRAM AC-*
> *QUISIVIT CULTUI CHRISTIANO, CUIUS ANIMA*
> *REGNET CUM CHRISTO. AMEN.*
>
> (Here lies Duke Godfrey de
> Bouillon, who acquired all this
> land for the Christian religion;
> may his soul reign with Christ. Amen.)

> *REX BALDUINUS, JUDAS ALTER MACHABEUS,*
> *SPES PATRIAE, VIGOR ECCLESIAE, VIRTUS UTRIUSQUE,*
> *QUEM FORMIDABANT, CUI DONA TRIBUTA FEREBANT*
> *CEDAR ET AEGYPTUS, DAN AC HOMICIDA DAMASCUS.*
> *PROH DOLOR! IN MODICO CLAUDITUR HOC TUMULO.*
>
> (King Baldwin, another Judas the Maccabee,
> hope of the Fatherland, strength of the Church,
> and the courage of both, to whom gifts as tribute were brought by
> Kedar and from Egypt, Dan and murderous Damascus.
> Alas for grief! He is enclosed in this mean tomb.)

The Holy Sepulchre, after U.Halbreiter, 1846

Western powers did not react until the middle of the nineteenth century. In 1846 a new Pope, Pius IX, was elected. The following year he appointed a Latin Patriarch of Jerusalem, an office dormant since the Middle Ages. In 1850 the French Ambassador at Istanbul, General Aupick, speaking for France, and also Austria, Belgium, Sardinia and Spain, demanded for the Franciscans all they had possessed before 1757, the Rotunda, the Edicule, the Stone of Unction, the Seven Arches of the Virgin, the Prison of

Christ, the Courtyard of the Holy Sepulchre, the Church of the Assumption, and the Church of the Nativity at Bethlehem. This was bitterly opposed by Russia on behalf of the Greek Orthodox, and the Tsar threatened to withdraw his ambassador if the Sultan gave way.

The Sultan appointed a committee to study the question. It rejected the Latin claims totally, and recommended that the *Status Quo* of 1757 be strictly maintained. The result—with other causes—was the Crimean War. Paradoxically, it was ended by the Treaty of Paris, which all the powers signed, undertaking to maintain the *status quo ante bellum*. As a *douceur*, France was given the Crusader Church of St Anne. Sultan Abdul-Majid further confirmed the *Status Quo* by *firmans* in 1868 and 1869, while in 1878 the Treaty of Vienna, which concluded the Russo-Turkish War, specified that no change be made in the *Status Quo*.

At the end of the Great War of 1914–18 a Mandate over Palestine was granted to Great Britain. The Treaty of Versailles provided for a commission to produce a Constitution for the Holy Places, but no agreement was ever reached on its composition. Thus the *Status Quo* as it existed in 1757, and as confirmed in 1852 by *firman*, and subsequent *firmans*, continued in force. In 1948 the Mandatory Power, Great Britain, under a Labour Government, renounced the Mandate over Palestine. The country, following war between the new State of Israel and neighbouring Arab powers, was divided between Israel and Jordan, by whom the *Status Quo* was faithfully observed. The same has been the case since 1967, when, following the Six-Day War, the Old City fell to Israel, which since then has observed the *Status Quo* with the same scrupulousness.

In 1927 an earthquake and in 1934 a disastrous fire, which burnt the dome above the Rotunda, caused very severe damage, but agreement could not be reached between the communities in regard to repairs. The Mandatory Power thus exercised the right of intervention that the Ottoman Turkish *firman* had envisaged. The Rotunda was shored up with scaffolding, the Director of Antiquities of the day remarking that the scaffolding was such as to last for a hundred years. At the same time the façade of the south front was shored up, that otherwise would have collapsed through age. In 1934 the Latin Patriarch proposed the total demolition of all the buildings, and a new construction that would provide each community with a separate section in

Latin Easter ceremonies

which to perform its own liturgy. A plan of this kind was published in 1949 by Archbishop, later Cardinal, Testa, with the aid of Dominican and French scholars. It also proposed a seventh community, a separate chapel being provided in the plan for the Anglican rite. In 1955 an international conference of architects took place, which led to the creation of a Common Technical Bureau of Armenian, French and Greek architects in 1959. Work began in 1961, with soundings throughout the building, the whole of which was stabilised. The work continued until 1977, when it was decided that the total renovation of the dome over the Rotunda was necessary. It was difficult to find persons of the right experience in Jerusalem, and a British team of contractors and designers brought out steelworkers, concrete sprayers, plasterers, welders and lead workers. A system of wrought-iron arches and a very thin reinforced concrete shell, only 115 mm. thick, support the load. The interior is lined with plaster which can be decorated either with frescoes or mosaics. There is no wood. In accordance with tradition, the exterior is of lead. All this work was completed in 1980. The reason why there is still scaffolding in the interior of the dome is that the three communities have not yet decided whether it should be decorated with fresco or with mosaic. The latter would be the choice in accordance with tradition (see above, p.19).

PART TWO: VISIT

I. The Entrance and South Courtyard

The original entrance to the Basilica is largely masked by the shops in the Suq al-Attarin, the continuation of the Suq Khan ez-Zeit, and only some elements of it can be seen. After the Eighth Station of the Cross, on the right, is a stone staircase, with, at the top, a winding street which leads to the Coptic Patriarchal *Cathedral of St Antony*, and an adjacent Coptic *Chapel of St Helena*. At the doorway to the convent a shaft of a column marks the Ninth Station. On the left is another doorway which leads to a terrace, with, in its centre, the dome of the *Chapel of St Helena* in the Basilica, and, behind it, the exterior of the Crusader ambulatory. Among the ruins of the Augustinian convent are the very small cells inhabited by the Ethiopian monks, to which they withdrew in 1660. This terrace is, in fact, the floor level of Constantine's *Martyrion* and its atrium. On the far side is the Ethiopian *Chapel of the Four Living Creatures*, and, below, a Coptic *Chapel of St Michael the Archangel*. The Ethiopian buildings are scrupulously clean and tidy, in sharp contrast to the adjacent Coptic ones. The latter are known as the *Deir al-Sultan*, the Sultan's Monastery, because it was donated to them by Saladin. It is sadly neglected, unlike the Coptic churches and monasteries in Egypt. The monks here are from the Monastery of St Antony the Hermit, the oldest of all monasteries, which is situated in the Eastern Desert near the Red Sea.

Returning to the Suq Khan ez-Zeit, there is a shabby-looking sweet and coffee shop marked *Zalatimo*. At the back, where there is an untidy store, one can look through a hole in the wall at some of the tumbled remains of Constantine's main entrance.

(opposite) *General view of the Basilica of the Holy Sepulchre*

Entrance to the basilica

Farther along the street, turning first right, and then left, one reaches the Russian Mission in Exile, open 9 a.m. to 3 p.m. on weekdays, but not during the Orthodox Holy Week. This is a late nineteenth century building in red brick, which masks elements of the Constantinian entrance to the Basilica. It was acquired by Russia in 1859. In 1882 the area was excavated at the expense of the Grand Duke Serge Alexandrovitch, whence the building is known as the St Alexander Nevsky Hospice. Some remains of an arch erected in the time of Hadrian can be seen, and a wall which re-uses large stone blocks of the time of Herod. Probably this was built as part of the Hadrianic temple. A doorway is shown which is known popularly as the Gate of Judgement, through which it is alleged that Christ passed on the way to Calvary. It is almost certainly of the fourth century.

A small charge is made for entry.

Returning to the street, we proceed up the Suq ed-Dabbagha. On the left is the Lutheran Church of the Redeemer, built on the foundation of the Church of St Mary la Latine, built for western pilgrims in 1063, and wholly rebuilt by German Lutherans in 1898. A fine view of the whole of the exterior of the Basilica of the Holy Sepulchre can be obtained from the tower.

Proceeding onward up the street, a small doorway leads into the South Courtyard of the Holy Sepulchre. The bases of columns that once supported a portico can be seen. The

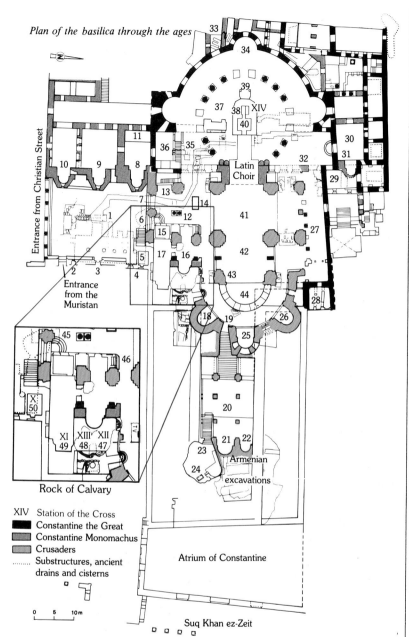

Plan of the basilica through the ages

Entrance from Christian Street

Entrance from the Muristan

Latin Choir

Armenian excavations

Atrium of Constantine

Rock of Calvary

XIV Station of the Cross
■ Constantine the Great
▨ Constantine Monomachus
▨ Crusaders
.... Substructures, ancient drains and cisterns

0   5   10 m

Suq Khan ez-Zeit

1. Southern atrium; 2. Monastery of Abraham; 3. Armenian Chapel of St James; 4. Coptic Chapel of St Michael the Archangel; 5. Chapel of St Mary of Egypt; 6. Tomb of Philippe d'Aubigny; 7. Main door; 8. Chapel of the Forty Martyrs; 9. Chapel of St Mary Magdalen; 10. Greek Chapel of St James; 11. Belfry; 12. Tomb of Godfrey de Bouillon; 13. Bench for Muslim doorkeepers; 14. Stone of Anointing; 15. Greek Sacristy; 16. Chapel of Adam; 17. Greek Treasury; 18. Chapel of the Derision; 19. Stairway and carved pilgrims' crosses; 20. Crusader Chapel of St Helena (now Armenian Chapel of St Gregory the Illuminator); 21. Altar of St Gregory; 22. Altar of St Dismas; 23. Chapel of the Finding of the Cross; 24. Statue of St Helena; 25. Chapel of the Parting of the Raiment; 26. Chapel of St Longinus; 27. Arches of the Virgin; 28. Prison of Christ; 29. Latin Sacristy; 30. Chapel of the Apparition; 31. Column of Flagellation; 32. Chapel of St Mary Magdalen; 33. Tombs of Joseph of Arimathaea and Nicodemus; 34. Chapel of St Nicodemus (Syrian Orthodox); 35. Place of the Three Maries; 36. Armenian divan; 37. Rotunda; 38. Edicule of the Holy Sepulchre; 39. Coptic Chapel; 40. Chapel of the Angel; 41. 'Navel' of the World; 42. Greek Choir (Katholikon); 43. Throne of the Patriarch of Jerusalem; 44. Altar; 45, 46. Stairs up to Calvary; 47. Greek Altar of the Crucifixion; 48. Latin Altar of *Stabat Mater*; 49. Latin Altar of the Nailing to the Cross; 50. Latin Chapel of the Franks

Monastery of Abraham

paved courtyard is used once a year by the Greek Orthodox
Patriarch for the ceremony of the Washing of the Feet on
their Maundy Thursday. On the left of the courtyard are
three chapels belonging to the Greeks: *St James's*, used for
the Byzantine-Arab rite, and containing Crusader tombs; *St
John's*, on the site of the original baptistery; and the *Forty
Martyrs*. The present decorations are quite modern.

There is a very large cistern under the courtyard. On the
right hand side is the Greek Convent of Abraham, with a
huge cistern known as St Helen's underneath. Upstairs is

the *Chapel of Abraham,* in which Anglicans can celebrate after application to the Greek Patriarch through their Bishop in Jerusalem. All that is necessary is provided. The chapel commemorates Abraham's sacrifice of a ram caught in a thicket in the place of his son, Isaac, the prototype of the sacrifice of Christ. Next to the Greek Convent is the Armenian *Chapel of St John,* and then the Coptic Chapel of *St Michael the Archangel.*

The façade of the Basilica is typical of twelfth century French building. Formerly there was an elaborate tympanum over the two doors. It had been very badly damaged by the weather, and was removed to the Rockefeller Museum to prevent its total disintegration. The right hand door was walled up by Saladin: since 1246 two Muslim families have been custodians of the left hand door. It is opened with elaborate ceremony at 4 a.m. daily, and closed again at 8 p.m., by the three sacristans of the major communities, Armenian, Greek and Latin. On the right of the door a wooden cover can be raised to display the tomb of Philippe d'Aubigny, Governor of Jersey and tutor of King Henry III of England. He came to Palestine in 1222, and accompanied the Emperor Frederick II to Jerusalem in 1228 (see above, p.38).

In the corner on the left of the courtyard is a belfry, built in 1160 to 1180 by Maître Jourdain. The top storey collapsed in 1549, but was roofed with red tiles only in 1719. In the right hand corner a flight of steps leads to a small building which was once the entrance to Calvary when it was an independent building. It is now the *Chapel of Our Lady of Sorrows,* or *of the Franks.* It belongs exclusively to the Latins. Underneath it is the small Greek Orthodox *Oratory of St Mary of Egypt,* which commemorates her conversion to Christianity in the atrium of the Basilica.

II. Calvary and the Chapel of Adam

Immediately on the right of the entrance a staircase leads to Calvary. A second staircase was added in 1810 by the Greeks behind the blocked doorway. The platform is raised 14′8″ (4.5 m.) above the floor of the church, and measures 37′6″ × 30′9″ (11.45 × 9.25 m.), and is divided into two naves by two large pillars. The right hand nave belongs to the Latins, the left hand to the Greeks.

The right hand altar, of silver plate, was the gift of Ferdinand de Medici, Grand Duke of Tuscany, and originally

Crusader mosaic of the Ascension, medallion in the ceiling of the Latin chapel on Calvary

Latin Altar of the Nailing to the Cross (11th Station)

intended for the Stone of Anointing (below, p.52). It was the
work of Fr Dominic Portigiani, OP, of St Mark's Convent,
Florence, in 1588. Six panels depict scenes from the Passion.

A Crusader description of the chapel records that the
whole of it was decorated with mosaic, but of this the figure
of Christ in the centre of the ceiling is all that remains.
The rest of the mosaics and marble panelling were erected
in 1937. They show Jesus being nailed to the Cross with
the Holy Women standing by, and Abraham's sacrifice of a
ram in substitution for his son Isaac.

To the left of this altar is a small altar, also the property
of the Latins, of Our Lady of Sorrows. The small bust was
the gift of Queen Maria I Braganza of Portugal, and brought
from Lisbon in 1778. It shows a sword of grief piercing her
heart. Part of the Rock of Calvary is exposed under this
altar. In this chapel the Latins celebrate the Tenth to
Thirteenth Stations of the Cross, the first nine having been
commemorated outside. The *Tenth Station of the Cross*,
Jesus is stripped of his garments, is commemorated at the
head of the stairs. The *Eleventh Station* is commemorated at
the silver altar, where the mosaic shows Jesus being nailed
to the Cross. The *Thirteenth Station*, Jesus is taken down

*Altar of Our Lady of Sorrows (*Stabat Mater*)—13th Station of the Cross*

from the Cross, is commemorated at the altar of Our Lady of Sorrows.

For the *Twelfth Station*, Jesus dies upon the Cross, one crosses over to the left hand side, where a Greek altar stands on a small platform. Here the white limestone rock of Calvary is exposed under plate glass. Under this altar is a disc with an opening in the centre, covering the place where the Cross stood. On the two sides of the altar are black discs where the crosses of the two thieves are believed to have stood. On the right of the altar a metal plate covers a great rent in the rock. This is believed to have been caused by the earthquake at the time of Christ's death. It is approximately 6" (15 cm.) wide, and visible also in the Chapel of Adam below Calvary. This chapel commemorates the ancient parallelism between Adam, the first man, in whom the whole human race first sinned, and the new Adam, Christ, in whom all are made alive.

Excavation here in 1977 shows that the remains of the rock of Calvary, or Golgotha, was roughly kidney-shaped. The remains of walls were found of the Crusader, Byzantine and pre-Constantinian periods, presumably of the small shrine of Aphrodite (above, p.10). Here ashes and calcined bones, from former sacrifices, were found, together with coins of the first half of the third century and associated pottery. So too was a small pagan altar of offering. All this evidence, taken together, points both to the accuracy of the report of St Jerome that this was a pagan shrine in honour of Aphrodite, and therefore to the authenticity of the site as the place of the Crucifixion.

The name Golgotha is from the Aramaic *golgoltā*, meaning a skull. Just as Arabs today use the word *rās*, head, to mean any rocky projection, not necessarily head-shaped, so *golgoltā* need only mean a rocky projection, not necessarily skull-shaped. As early as Origen (185–254) the tradition of the burial of Adam here existed: he say, 'Because of the place of the skull we heard that the Hebrews have a tradition that Adam lies buried there.' Epiphanius (315–403) likewise knew the tradition: 'When Jesus Christ was crucified here ... he wet the bones of our first ancestor with his blood.' A similar line of thinking existed in Jewish tradition, which placed the grave of Adam beneath the altar of burnt-offering. Later the tradition was moved, giving him a burial in Hebron beside the Patriarchs. Origen's 'Hebrews' should rather be thought of as Hebrew Christians, who transformed an ancient legend and associated it with the Crucifixion. It was the whole of these associations which was important in the minds of Hadrian's temple-builders when they came to adapt the site to their own ends.

III. The Stone of Unction

At the foot of Calvary is the *Stone of Unction*, or of *Anointing*, a polished red stone approximately 18'6" long, 4'3" wide, and 11'6" high (5.70 × 1.30 × 0.30 m.). Here, according to tradition, the lifeless body of Christ was prepared and anointed for burial before it was placed in the tomb (John 19.38).

In Byzantine times there was an *Oratory of St Mary* here, which was demolished when the Crusaders reconstructed the church. About 39' (12 m.) away on the west side a stone slab

The Stone of Anointing

Pilgrims venerating the Stone of Anointing

surmounted by an iron cage marks the traditional spot where the three Maries stood during the Crucifixion. Possibly this is a commemoration that has been relocated from the site of the former oratory when the Stone of Unction was set up.

It is not possible to detail all the stages in the evolution of the ceremonies of Good Friday, of which at the end of the fourth century the nun Egeria gives such a moving description in her *Pilgrimage*. Already at this time, after appropriate readings, including that of the Passion according to St John, the faithful venerated the Wood of the Cross which the Bishop held in his hands for them. This took place on Golgotha. There could have been very little space for this veneration, and one may deduce that the people came in a long file. At this time only one flight of stairs led up to Calvary.

There is no ancient tradition where the body of Christ was prepared for burial. But by the tenth century St Ethelwold, Bishop of Winchester, records a Good Friday ceremony in which the Veneration of the Cross was followed by one of *depositio*, the taking down from the Cross and the ritual burial of a *Christus* figure. It is thought that this may have originated as early as the fifth century, but most probably in northern France or southern England. Ethelwold's practice would seem to connect it with the Royal Chapel of the Saxon Kings.

In the Greek rite the Burial of Christ is preceded by the sprinkling of rose leaves on an icon placed on the *Stone of Unction*. In the Latin rite a starkly realistic figure of Christ is taken down from a Cross. It has flexible shoulder joints, and with it are models of all the implements of the Passion, the Hammer, the Nails, and the Tongs with which the Nails were withdrawn from the lifeless body. There are silver sprinklers for rosewater, and two silver containers for herbs and spices. These silver objects are of seventeenth century Polish manufacture, as inscriptions show. None of the other objects bear any indication of date. However ancient the ceremony may be, it is improbable that any of the objects are earlier than the seventeenth century.

It was near here that the tombs of Godfrey de Bouillon and the Crusader kings formerly stood, and which were removed by the Greeks in 1810.

Behind the Stone of Unction is a splendid new mosaic erected by the Greek Orthodox Patriarchate in 1991, depicting the taking down from the Cross, the preparation of the Body for burial, and the carrying of the Body to the Tomb. The design of the rocks, and in particular the style and colouring of the pink rocks, are reminiscent of the style of Dominico Theotocopuli, commonly known as El Greco, the Cretan painter, architect and sculptor, who, after studies in Rome and Venice, became best known for the masterpieces he painted in Spain, where he died in Toledo in 1614.

IV. The Rotunda and the Tomb of Christ

Edicule of the Holy Sepulchre

Now entering the Rotunda, on the left is a door which opens on to the Armenian *divan*, or reception room, and close by stairs are to be seen leading to the gallery of the Rotunda. The wicket gate is kept locked, but generally the Armenian sacristan can be found, who readily will give permission to visitors to go up to the gallery. This is well worth doing, because it enables one to look down on the whole of the Rotunda, including the Edicule, and, at the same time

The Latin chapel

to get a clear view through the whole of church as far as the apse above the Greek altar.

There are two galleries in the Rotunda. The upper gallery belongs to the Greeks, the lower is divided between the Armenians and the Latins. The Armenians have two chapels at this level, and an attractive floor mosaic by a modern Italian artist.

The Rotunda itself has six square piers and ten pillars. The piers are arranged in pairs on the north, west and south. The pillars are between them in two sets of three on the western side, and in two pairs on the east. The space between them on the east is occupied by the massive triumphal arch built under Constantine IX Monomachus. Formerly the piers and pillars were all free standing. At least since 1810 the processional way on the outer circumference of the Rotunda has been encumbered with walls that divide the space into small rooms and stores. This outer circumference has three apses, on the north, west and south. The western apse is used as a chapel by the Syrian Jacobites, but their altar is used only on Sundays and certain festivals. Only then is it dressed. A short passage on the south-west side of the apse leads to two tombs of the type known as *kokhim*, and with pits for ossuaries, in accordance with Jewish first century practice. The two tombs are ascribed to Joseph of Arimathaea and to Nicodemus (above, p.45). They are, however, of great historical importance, in that they show that when they were constructed in the first century they were outside the city, in accordance with Jewish law relating to burial. They show too that the area was indeed an authentic burial ground.

In the north-west segment of the outer circumference a passage leads towards the well of the ancient Patriarchate, in fact a large cistern, not a well. This is the common property of all the communities, and access to it is available at all times. It was the sole water supply of ancient times.

The Edicule, or Tomb of Christ, stands in the centre of the Rotunda. A small raised platform runs between the Triumphal Arch and the Edicule, and is known as the Latin choir. Here, on certain festivals, the Greeks erect an altar, as do the Latins on the Feast of *Corpus Christi* and certain other occasions. This Latin altar, known as the Pontifical

Interior of the Edicule

Altar, is of the greatest magnificence, and indeed a work of art of real importance. It is of silver, and an inscription on it records that it was constructed at Lima, in Peru, in 1681. Similar silver altars are to be found in a number of churches in Andalucía and other parts of Spain. A particularly beautiful one is in the cathedral at Ronda. Like those in Spain, this altar has *en suite* a Crucifix and Tabernacle with candlesticks and jewelled silver and silver-gilt ornaments. The candlesticks have each a representation of Christ rising from the dead and the Edicule as it was before the fire of 1808. *En suite* likewise is the Tabernacle, with dancing angels on the side and the Lamb in front, in high relief; above is the Risen Christ, flanked by St Francis of Assisi and St Antony of Padua.

In front of the Edicule on either side is a low wall, on which stand candlesticks belonging severally to the Armenians, Greeks and Latins. They are lit according to whichever rite is being celebrated. On the front of the Edicule there are four rows of lamps. The top row belongs to the Latins, the bottom to the Armenians, and the two middle rows to the Greeks. The Edicule is 26′ long and 17$^1/_2$′ wide (8.30 × 5.90 m.), and consists of a hexagonal western part and an eastern addition. This last is known as the Angels' Chapel, that is, where the angels were found sitting, and is 11′ × 10′ (3.40 × 3.90 m.). In the centre is a pedestal, with a piece of the stone which was rolled in front when Jesus was buried. This pedestal serves as an altar when the Greeks celebrate. The Armenians and Latins celebrate on a *mensa* stretched across the funeral couch inside. The *Holy Sepulchre* properly so called is 6$^1/_2$′ × 6′ (2.07 × 1.93 m.). On the right hand side is a marble slab about 5′ × 2′ and 3′ high (2.02 × 0.93 m., × 0.66 m.) above the floor which marks the burial place of Christ. This was placed here in 1555 when the Edicule was reconstructed by Fr Boniface of Ragusa. He recorded that he deliberately made a cut in the marble so that the Turks should not steal it. The last person to see the actual funeral couch, Maximos Symaios in 1810, recorded that it had been greatly damaged by relic-hunters, and that what had been a flat bed had been hollowed out. Little, too, of the exterior walls remained except on the northern side.

There is almost always a press of people wishing to pray in this most sacred place. The space is very confined, and cannot admit more than four persons at any one time. For these reasons *it is customary not to spend more than three minutes in prayer in it.* It is also customary to place crucifixes,

Chapel of the Angel

rosaries and medals which have been blessed in the Basilica on the marble slab, which is kissed by many pilgrims.

The interior of the Edicule is lined with marble, and decorated with pictures, hangings, lamps and candelabra which are numerically divided between the three principal communities. This division is strictly defined by the *Status Quo*.

Behind the Edicule is the Chapel of the Copts. In 1048 Constantine IX Monomachus built a parochial altar here for the people of Jerusalem. The Crusaders kept it, calling it *Cavet* (Norman-French: head), because it stood at the head of the monument. The Copts have used it since the seventeenth century only.

Coptic Chapel

The Edicule which was destroyed by fire in 1808 was of no great antiquity. It was one which the Franciscan Custodian of the Holy Land, Boniface of Ragusa, had had built in 1555. After the fire of 1808 the Greeks rebuilt the Edicule without the Coptic Chapel; the latter was rebuilt only at the request of Muhammad Ali the Great, Khedive of Egypt, somewhat later.

The Edicule of Boniface of Ragusa, decorated with plain marble panelling, was very austere in appearance. Its appearance is known to us from drawings made at the end of the sixteenth century. It had, nevertheless, the essential features of the present Edicule, the 16 small pillars, the division into two apartments, and the small cupola on top. A model of what it looked like in the tenth century is to be seen in a museum in Arles, but at that time the Chapel of the Angel had three open sides and a roof supported by two pillars in front. The hexagonal inner chamber, as seen from the outside, is a design of great antiquity, for it is shown as a hexagonal structure on glass pilgrim flasks which Professor Dan Barag has been able to determine belong to the sixth century. To this same century belongs an ivory in the Trivulzi Collection in Milan, and this shows that even then the Edicule was surmounted by a *tourelle*, or decorative cupola. Thus the present Edicule has preserved what are assuredly ancient features.

The earliest representation known of the Edicule is an ivory reliquary from Samagher, near Pola, in Istria, now in the Museo Archeologico in Venice (p.17). Scenes depicted on it enable Professora Margherita Guarducci to date it at 439. This is just over a century from when, as Eusebius tells us, that Constantine had the Edicule cut out from the surrounding rock. It was octagonal, with an eight-sided pyramidal roof. The same representations can be seen on pilgrim flasks preserved in the cathedrals at Monza and Bobbio, but with a Cross on top. They are in two dimensions, in relief.

At some time in the sixth century this Cross was replaced by a cupola, with a Cross on top. The original Rotunda was probably open to the sky at the top. Certain of its decorative features suggest that it had an *oculus*, or window open to the sky, as did many ancient funerary monuments, like the Pantheon in Rome. The cupola would protect the Edicule to some extent against rain. Perhaps also it protected a ventilation shaft, for otherwise the Edicule would have been without any ventilation.

Unfortunately no early source tells us how the Edicule was decorated, except that it had marble panelling. To this Eusebius adds that it was 'richly decorated', which suggests that it also had mosaics. It is extraordinary that almost all the funeral monuments of the Roman and Byzantine Emperors have perished. One would expect that the Edicule would have been modelled on one such. The most obvious example that springs to mind as of reasonably close date is the tomb of Galla Placidia in Ravenna, a very plain building now outside, but richly encrusted with mosaics within.

V. The Katholikon or Greek Cathedral

As has been explained, in 1808–10 the Greeks set up high walls in the Crusader choir and a high iconostasis of stone, completely cutting off the centre of the basilica for their own use. This action wholly destroyed the unity of the building. During the recent restorations these walls have been taken down and rebuilt, so that for a short while it was possible to see the original intentions of the Crusaders, as interpreted by Maître Jourdain, their architect. At the present the walls remain with virgin whiteness, but it is probable that they may once again be covered with icons and other paintings, as before.

A cupola covers the western part of the church. Under the cupola there is a small marble hemisphere, which marks the so-called centre of the world, on the basis of a verse of Psalm 74 (73):12:

> Yet God my King is from of old,
> working salvation in the midst of the earth,

an idea reflected in a different context by Ezekiel 5:5:

> Thus says the Lord God: This is Jerusalem; I have set her in the centre of the nations, with countries round about her.

If the legend is of antiquity, the marble representation probably does not antedate the restoration of 1810. A map of 1580 depicts Jerusalem as the centre of the world, joining the three continents of Europe, Asia and Africa. Remote and separate is America Terranova, and, in the far north, separate from Europe, England and Scandinavia.

The stalls of the Greek choir belong to the most recent restoration, but the two Pontifical Thrones, on the north for the Patriarch of Antioch and on the south for the Patriarch of Jerusalem, belong to the 1810 restoration.

The Greeks and other Orthodox, Armenian, Coptic, Ethiopian, and Syrian Jacobite, follow the old Julian Calendar which, for the Latins, was replaced by the Gregorian Calendar in 1582. The Orthodox ceremonies of Easter fall on the Sunday after the first full Moon of Spring, and thus can occur either before or after the Latin Easter. They very rarely coincide. The Greek ceremonies have been described many times, and most notably by H.V.Morton, *In the Steps of the Master*. The ceremonies begin in the atrium on Maundy Thursday with the Washing of the Feet by the Patriarch, a

The Katholikon before the re-erection of the Iconostasis

ceremony shared by other Orthodox, but not the Armenians, who have their own ceremony in St James's Cathedral. There are lengthy services on Good Friday, which culminate in a ceremonial burial of an icon of Christ. The most elaborate and celebrated of these ceremonies is that on Easter Eve, during which all lamps are extinguished, so that the crowd that has gathered for the occasion is left in total darkness. Orthodox clergy have already proceeded to the Edicule, on this occasion including the Armenian Patriarch. The people wait in the utmost suspense for the kindling of the Holy Fire, which takes place within the Edicule. The moment of the

Congregation at the ceremony of the Holy Fire

Resurrection is proclaimed by the passing of a candle, lit from the New Fire, through an aperture in the side of the Edicule, which is believed popularly, but wholly erroneously, to have come down from heaven. This has never been asserted by the Orthodox authorities. An indescribable tumult follows, the crowd all struggling to light their own tapers and to carry them to their own homes, where all lights and fires have been extinguished in preparation for the ceremony. There is a superstition that this fire will not burn human beings, and some of the faithful allow the fire to play on their own bodies.

The ceremony is claimed to date from the Apostolic Age, but is first mentioned in literature in the ninth century.

VI. The Franciscan Chapels and the Ambulatory

The western side of the Rotunda has transepts on the north and south, walled off from the former processional way round the outer perimeter of the pillars of the Rotunda. The southern end, in Armenian possession, has already been described (above, p.55). The northern end, in Latin possession, is known as the *Chapel of the Apparition*, or the *Appearance of the Risen Christ to St Mary Magdalen*, or simply *St Mary Magdalen's Chapel*, and has a modern altar set up against a pier on the eastern side. This chapel is used by the Franciscans for certain ceremonies, including visits by the Latin Patriarch, and for Mass for larger parties of pilgrims. It formerly had a pavement that had been constructed at the time of the restoration of Constantine IX Monomachus, but it was removed in 1968 as an archaeological relic, and set down again in a gallery. Further excavation at this time revealed building of the period of Constantine the Great and of Hadrian.

At the northern end of the chapel steps lead up to a splendid pair of new bronze doors, the gift of the people of Australia, in 1982. They are decorated with panels in relief, and with the arms of the Franciscans and of the Holy Land. These last, consisting of Five Crosses, in commemoration of the Five Wounds of Christ, were the personal Arms of Godfrey de Bouillon.

Within is the Franciscan Chapel of the *Apparition*, or *Appearance of the Risen Christ to His Mother*. This has recently been entirely redecorated and modernized; formerly the *décor* was in the manner of a nineteenth century Italian church. The altar and Tabernacle are the work of Fr Andrea Martini, OFM, of Rome; and the beautiful mosaic in the apse is the work of two Jewish mosaicists resident in Jerusalem, Mr and Mrs Sabi, as a happy augury of irenical friendship between Jews and Christians. The Tabernacle in the centre of the Cross is in the form of a globe. So the Constantinian tradition of mosaic has been maintained in a modern form.

On the southern side of the altar is a fragment of a porphyry column $29^1/_4''$ (0.75 m.) high. This is known as the *Column of Flagellation*, to which Jesus Christ was bound when he was scourged by the Roman soldiers. It has stood here since the tenth century, before which it was probably in the former church on Sion. Although the chapel is in the

Altar of St Mary Magdalen

hands of the Franciscans, other communities have the right
to come to venerate the column and to incense it.

This chapel is the only part of the church in which the
Blessed Sacrament is reserved. Benediction of the Blessed
Sacrament takes place here daily at the conclusion of the
Franciscan Procession, which begins at 4 p.m. Originally this
chapel was not part of the building, but the open courtyard
of the Patriarchate. On the far side there is access to a further
chapel of indeterminate date, which is thought to be a former
refectory. The private quarters of the Franciscan convent are
above.

In the corner on the eastern side of the *Chapel of the*

Appearance of the Risen Christ to St Mary Magdalen, commonly called the *St Mary Magdalen Chapel*, a door leads to the Franciscan Sacristy. A priest is always on duty here or nearby for confessions or other needs of the faithful.

In the sacristy, on the left, is a glass case on the wall which contains a pair of spurs and a sword with a scabbard, which are said to be those of Godfrey de Bouillon. There is also a pectoral Cross. These are used in creating Knights of the Holy Sepulchre. There are three separate, and conflicting, accounts of this ceremony as it was in the fifteenth century, showing that even then it had no wholly set ritual. In the first, after Mass at midnight, a knight gave the accolade five times in honour of the Five Wounds of Christ, and then once in honour of St George. Then the sword was delivered, naked, to the new knight 'in honour and reverence of God and of my lord St George.' The new knight then took an oath to guard the Holy Church, to help recover the Holy Land, to defend his own folk and keep justice, to keep his marriage holy, and to protect widows and orphans. In a second form the new knight was girded with the sword and spurs were used in the same way, the new knight swearing to be 'God's Knight', and to protect widows, orphans, the Church, and the poor; and to keep justice and to right wrongs 'so help me God and the Holy Sepulchre.' The oath was taken kneeling, after which the new knight was struck on the shoulder, with the words: 'Arise, knight, in honour of the Holy Sepulchre and the Knight St George.' In modern times a more elaborate ceremony takes place.

Leaving the sacristy and going behind the altar of the *St Mary Magdalen*, along the northern side of the Katholikon, there is a long gallery with seven pillars, known as the *Arches of the Virgin*. It is not clear why they have this name. Part of the construction appears to belong to the Crusader period, as certainly does the upper part, but the first four courses of the wall belong to the period of Constantine the Great. The central four columns and perhaps part of the last pier may have belonged to Constantine's Triportico.

At the extreme end of the gallery is a Greek chapel known as the *Prison of Christ*. Here tradition has it that Jesus and the two thieves were detained before their crucifixion. There are two round holes, said to be the stocks in which the feet of Jesus were fastened. Two impressions on the stone are said to be imprints of his feet. The legend, of Greek origin, does not antedate the fifteenth century. The origin

The 'Prison of Christ'

and purpose of this chapel is obscure. Among views that have been held is that it was a synagogue.

In the thick wall of the ambulatory behind the apse of the Katholikon are three apsidal chapels. The first is of *St Longinus*, the Roman soldier who pierced the side of Jesus after his death, 'and immediately there came out blood and water.' This belongs to the Greeks. Next is the Armenian chapel of the *Division of the Raiment*, in commemoration of the division of the garments of Jesus among the soldiers and the casting of lots for his seamless garment. The third chapel is of the *Derision* or *Crowning with Thorns*, and also belongs to the Greeks. In the centre is a box-like altar, which contains the so-called Column of Derision, a fragment of stone about 1' (0.30 m.) high. It is first recorded in 1384, and its size and colour, now light grey, are said to have changed several times since then. Between the first two of these altars is a door, which was originally provided to give access from the former Augustinian cloister.

VII. The Chapels of St Helena and the Invention of the Cross

Between the second and third chapels in the ambulatory a flight of twenty-nine steps leads down to the *Chapel of St Helena*, originally the crypt of Constantine's *Martyrion*. It is 65′ long and 42′ wide (20 × 12.9 m.). The whole belongs to the Armenians. The dome in the centre is carried by four ancient monolithic pillars with clumsy capitals, but the vaulting shows it to be of the twelfth century. There is a tradition that these columns used to shed tears—presumably condensation. The northern altar was dedicated to the Penitent Thief, and the centre altar to St Helena, but the Armenians now hold it in honour of their national saint, St Gregory the Illuminator. A seat on the right adjoining this altar is said to have been the one used by St Helena while the Cross was being excavated, a legend not older than the fifteenth century.

On the right thirteen steps lead to the *Chapel of the Invention* (or *Finding*) *of the Cross*. On either side of the stairs are numerous crosses incised at the time of the Crusades. On the right at the bottom is a marble slab with a Cross belonging to the Greeks. The altar belongs to the Latins. On 7 May, the Feast of the Invention of the Cross, Pontifical Mass is celebrated here by the Franciscan Custodian of the Holy Land, who carries here one of the Relics of the Cross

Chapel of St Helena

and places it above the altar. Behind the altar is a large bronze statue of St Helena, given by Archduke Maximilian of Austria, later Emperor of Mexico. On the right of the altar is a small cistern where the Cross of Jesus and those of the two thieves are said to have been found. Some traces of paintings of the Crusader period can be seen on the walls, but there is also much naked rock, with evidence of ancient quarrying.

Elsewhere, in the Latin rite, this feast day is kept on 3 May, and Jerusalem is an exception.

Crosses incised by Crusader pilgrims along the steps leading to the Chapel of the Finding of the Cross

Bibliographical Note

There is a very large literature on the Holy Sepulchre. Previous descriptions and plans have been superseded by V.C.Corbo, OFM, *Il Santo Sepolcro in Gerusalemme: aspetti archaeologici dalle origini al periodo crociato*, 3 vols, Franciscan Printing Press, Jerusalem, 1982, profusely illustrated with photographs, and plans. It includes a list of the principal works consulted, I, pp.17−19. In particular it supersedes much of C.Coüasnon, *The Church of the Holy Sepulchre in Jerusalem*, Schweich Lectures, British Academy (1972), OUP 1974. For the history of the building an invaluable mine of research is L.-H.Vincent, OP, and F.-M.Abel, OP, *Jérusalem Nouvelle*, 2 vols, Gabaldi, Paris, 1914, 1922, in spite of its age still the best work of its kind. There is much useful discussion in C.Kopp, *The Holy Places of the Gospels*, Eng.tr., Edinburgh & London, 1962. For the *Status Quo* an essential tool is Bishop Bernardin Collin, *Receuil de Documents concernant Jérusalem and les Lieux Saints*, Franciscan Printing Press, Jerusalem, 1982; a strictly impartial and balanced discussion of the political issues is W.Zander, *Israel and the Holy Places of Christendom*, Weidenfeld, London, 1971. There is much that is useful in E.Hoade, *Guide to the Holy Land*, 10th edn, Franciscan Printing Press, Jerusalem, 1979. F.Díez Fernandez, OSA, 'La recherche archéologique: la question de l'authenticité', in *Le Monde de la Bible*, Mars-Avril, no.33, Paris, 1984, is important for the only description so far of his excavations on Golgotha. In Greek, G.Labbas and T.Metropoulos, *Phriktòs Golgothâs*, (The Utter Horror of Golgotha), *Néa Sion*, Jerusalem, 1988, describe the most recent investigations. S.de Sandoli, *Chiesa del Santo Sepolcro: chiavi, porte, portinai*, Franciscan Printing Press, Jerusalem, 1986, is a fascinating account of rights of the major communities and the Muslim doorkeepers in the door of the church. J.Wilkinson, J.Hill and W.F.Ryan, *Jerusalem Pilgrimage, 1099−1185*, Hakluyt Society, 1988, is a collection of documents invaluable for the understanding of that period.

List of Illustrations